STAR OF BETHLEHEM

Matthew 2: 2

A brilliant star appeared in the sky on the night that Jesus was born. It guided the Three Kings to Bethlehem where Mary, Joseph and baby Jesus were sheltered in a stable.

*paper is colored on one side only,
egin with colored side of paper up.*

a.   Fold a paper square in half both
ays, as shown by the broken lines.
nfold the paper flat each time.

b.   TURN THE PAPER OVER

.   Fold the paper on the diagonal.
Unfold. Fold the paper on the other
iagonal, but do not unfold this time.

.   Hold the paper exactly as shown. Push your hands to each other until the paper forms a
riangle.

.   Arrange the four points of the paper into a three-dimensional star. Hang it from one point.

.   Star.

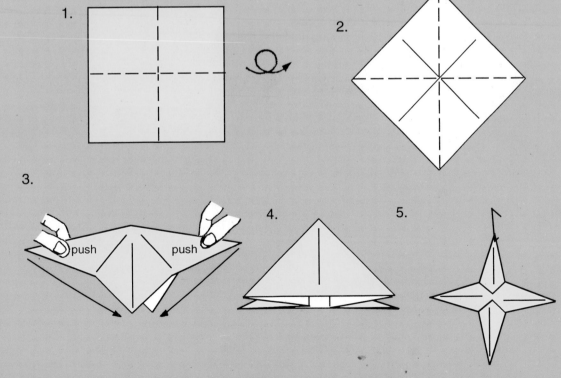

1.

ANGEL

Luke 2: 10 and many other references
Angels are spiritual beings who serve as God's messengers to protect people on earth.

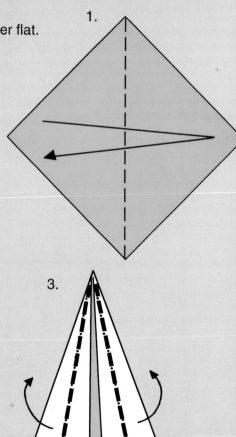

If paper is colored on one side only, begin with the colored side up.

1. Fold a paper square corner to corner. Unfold the paper flat.

2. Fold two outer EDGES to the middle.

3. Mountain fold the long edges to the BACK.

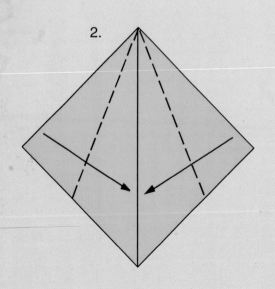

4. Flip the top layers out to the sides.

5. Unfold the paper flat.

6. Fold down the top corner a little and then fold it down again.

7. Fold the paper on the previous long creases. See the next drawing.

8. Shape the angel: Mountain fold the top corners, the shoulders and the bottom corner to the BACK.

9. Angel.

Standing Angel

The angel will stand up if you make a crease in the middle to bend the sides to the back.

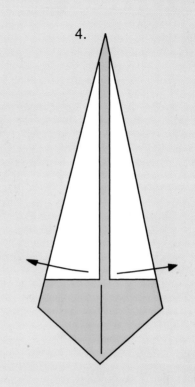

4.

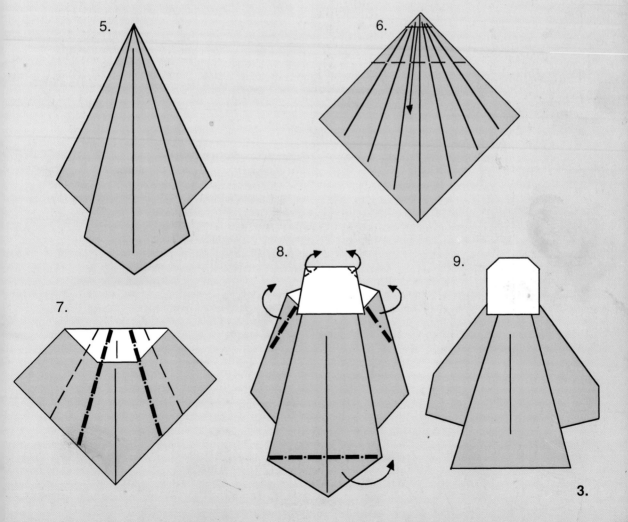

5.

6.

7.

8.

9.

3.

THE THREE KINGS

Matthew 2: 1-12

Three Oriental kings from the East travelled far to worship the newborn baby Jesus. They offered him precious gifts of gold, incense (frankincense) and rare fragrant oils (myrrh). The Three Kings are remembered at Christmas (December 25), but in some countries, the Day of the Three Kings is celebrated on January 6th.

You need:

3 origami paper squares in bright colors

Small Pieces of gold paper

Scissors, glue

Fold all three kings the same way.

If paper is colored on one side only, begin with colored side of paper up.

1. Fold the square in half.

2. Fold the corner to the folded edge; first on the front, then repeat on the back.

3. Fold the side over at an angle; first on the front, then repeat on the back.

4. Fold up the bottom corners of the robe to make a stand.

5. Cut a crown from gold paper and glue it to the king.

6. King.

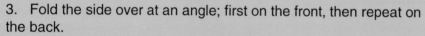

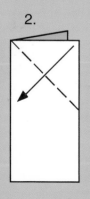

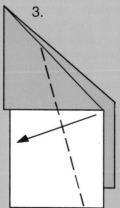

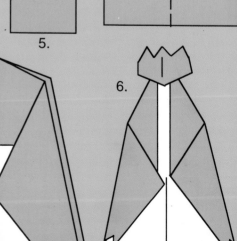

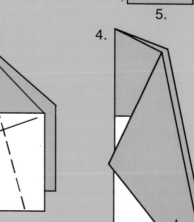

4.

FISH

Matthew 15: 32-37

The fish is an important symbol of Christianity. Fish was a staple food in Biblical times and is mentioned many times in the New Testament. The story of the loaves and fishes is especially well known. Several of Jesus' disciples were fishermen and when they left their trade to join Him in His teachings he called them "fishers of men." In addition, the Greek word for fish, Ichthus, became a secret password for early Christians. Its letters represent the abbreviation for "Jesus Christ God's Son Savior." "I" or "J" for Jesus "CH" for Christ, "THU" for God's son and "S" for Savior.

1. Fold a paper square corner to corner. Unfold paper flat.

2. Fold two EDGES to the crease.

3. Fold the two short edges to the middle.

4. Fold the paper in half.

5. Fold the front corner up and wrap it around with four small creases. Tuck it inside.

6. Fold up the tail.

7. Fish.

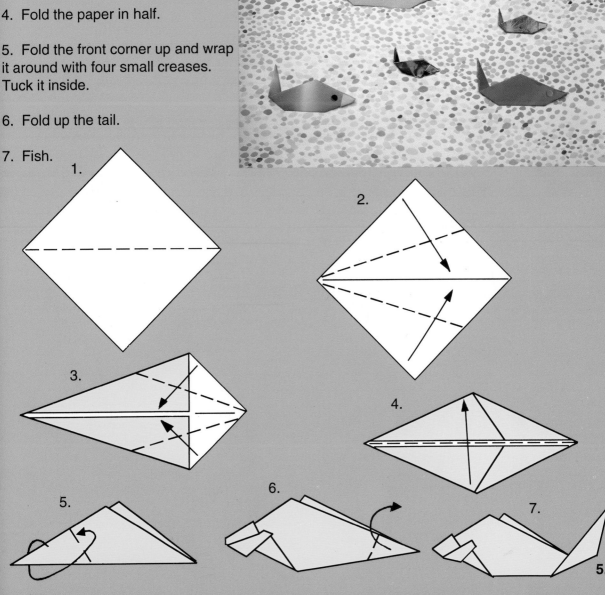

5.

CROSS

Mark 8: 34, Luke 9: 23

The Cross is the most important Christian symbol. It reminds us of the crucifixion of Jesus Christ and his redemption. The Cross is seen on church altars, carried in processions, used by bishops to give their blessings and worn as jewelry. Here you can find out how to make a Cross with a paper square which you can then use as a gift or greeting card.

Use a paper square colored on one side and white on the other. Begin with the colored side of the paper up.

1. Fold a paper square in quarters.

2. Fold the four loose corners in, not all the way to the opposite corner.

3. Unfold the paper flat.

4. Place the colored side up. Fold the four corners in on the creased lines.

1.

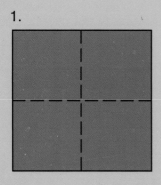

2.

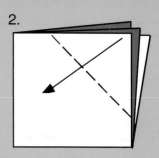

3.

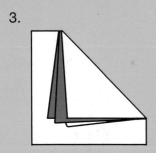

4.

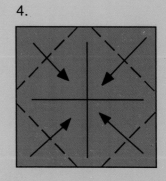

6.

5. TURN THE PAPER OVER.

6. Fold in THREE blunted corners, not all the way to the middle.

7. Turn the paper over again.

8. Cross.

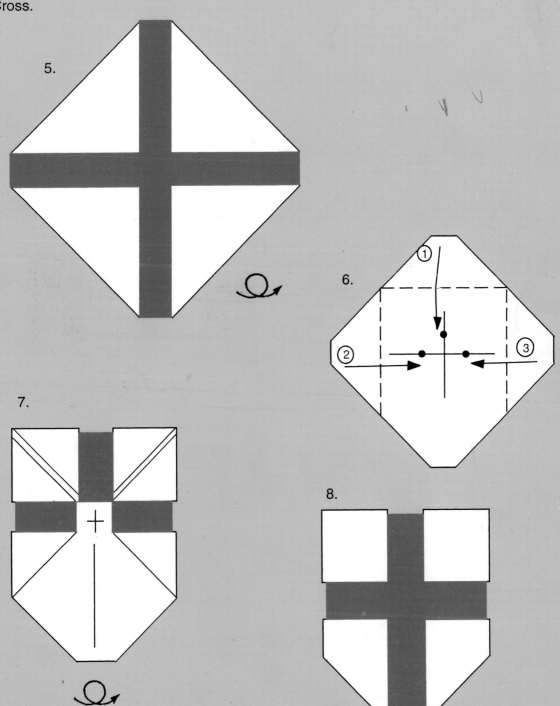

EASTER FLOWER

Luke 24: 35

At Easter Jesus rose from the dead. When flowers bloom in the spring they symbolize the spirit of renewed life after a long winter.

1a. Fold a paper square on the dotted lines shown. Unfold each time.

1b. TURN THE PAPER OVER

2. Fold the paper in half. Unfold. Fold in half the other way, but do not unfold.

3. Hold paper exactly as shown and push it together into a square with two flaps on each side. If you have three flaps on one side, flip one over.

4. Place the paper with the closed corner pointing to you. Fold the EDGES of two flaps on the front to the middle. Turn the paper over and repeat on the back.

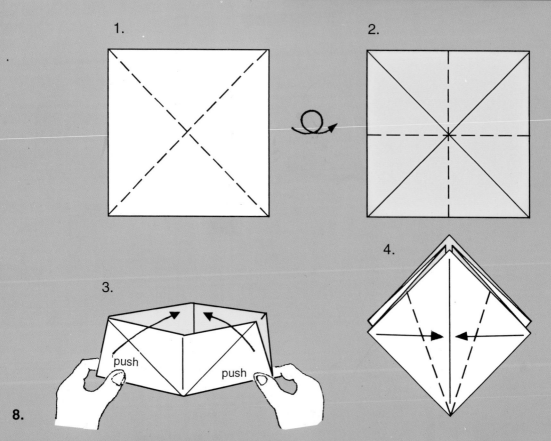

1.

2.

3.

push   push

4.

8.

5. Hold the paper at "X" with one hand. With the other hand pull down one layer of paper.
Push down on the middle of the flower and flatten it in the middle.

6. Easter Flower.

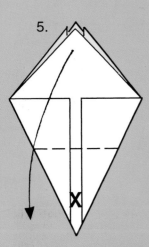

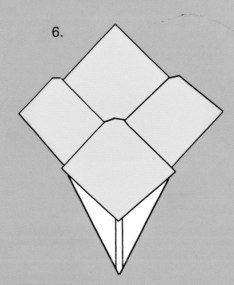

Stemmed Flower

You can make a three-dimensional flower for bouquets. In step 5 open the petals but do not
flatten them. Curve each one by stroking it between your thumb and forefinger, from the middle
out, or by rolling it over a pencil or toothpick. For a stem, tape on a pipe cleaner, chenille stem,
or drinking straw. Tape on leaves cut from green paper.

Large Easter Flower

Insert a small pink or yellow Easter flower into the center of a big white flower to create larger
bouquets as shown in the photograph on page 8.

CHURCH

Matthew 16: 18

Churches are houses of worship. They are often topped by high steeples which point towards God's domain in Heaven.

1. Fold the first three steps of the Star on page 1. Make sure you have two flaps on each side of the triangle. If not, then move one flap over. On the front, fold the outside corners up to the top corner. Turn the paper over and repeat on the back.

2. On the front, poke your finger in between the two layers of paper. Bring the top corner to the bottom corner, forming a square. Perform this step on both sides of the front. Then turn the paper over and repeat on the back.

3. Fold the right side over to the left, like a book page. Turn the paper over. Again fold the right side over to the left.

4. Fold the straight outside edges to the middle, first on the front and then on the back.

1.

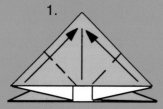

2.

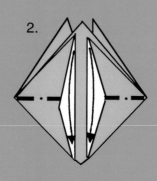

3.

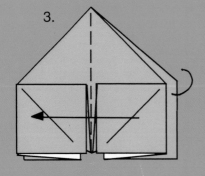

4.

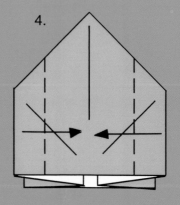

Again, fold the right side over to the left, like a book page. Turn the paper over and repeat on the back.

On the left, slide your finger in between the two layers on the front; push down on the top and flatten it. See next drawing. Repeat on the right side.

Fold up the bottom corner. Repeat steps 6 and 7 on the back.

Church.

Variations

The church stands up. You can draw on or cut paper into windows, a cross and other decorations.

5.

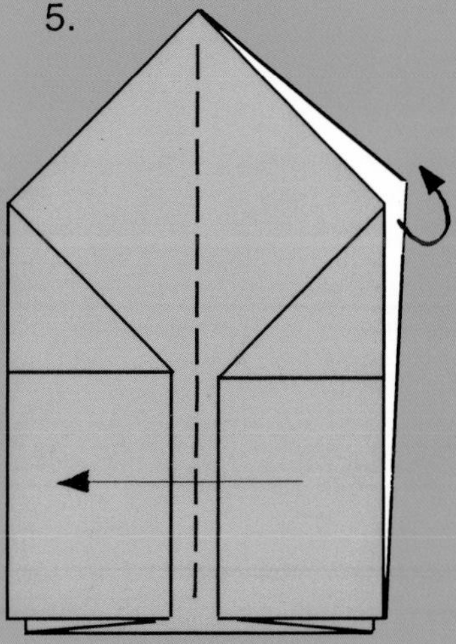

6.

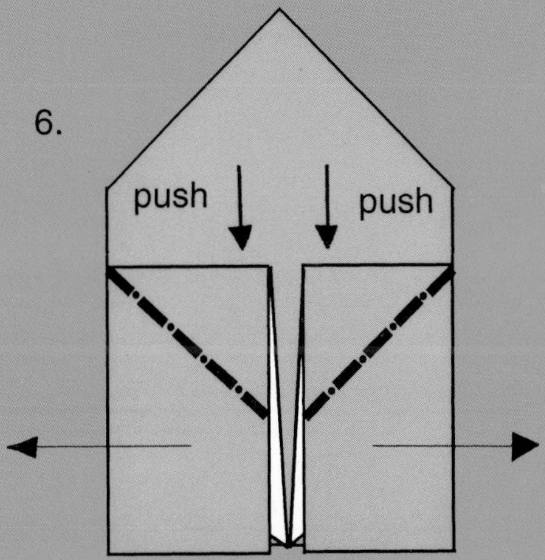

push   push

7.

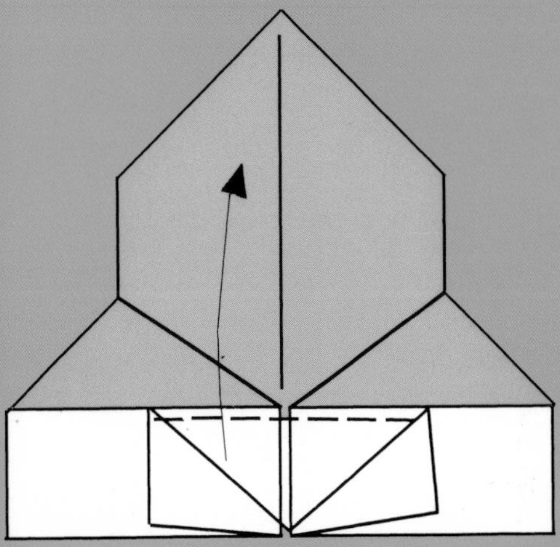

8.

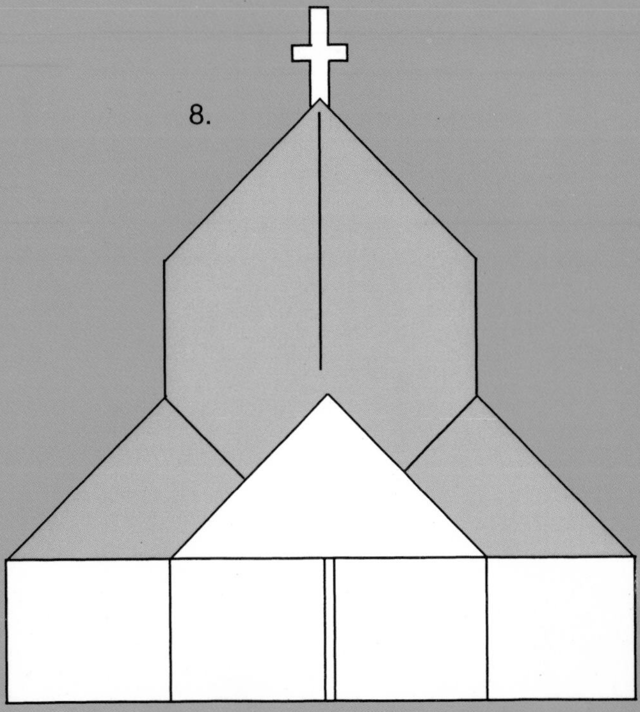

WHAT YOU CAN DO WITH ORIGAMI

It's fun to fold paper into figures which illustrate Bible stories, but you can also use them in practical ways. Here are a few ideas:

Greeting Cards:

Fold a piece of construction paper into quarters. Glue an origami on the front. Send cards for holidays, birthdays, parties and any other festive occasions.

Bookmarks:

Cut wide strips of construction paper. Fold them in half for extra strength. Glue an origami to the top.

Mobiles:

Origami are ideal for mobiles because they are very light. Pierce them at the top and tie a piece of thread, fishing line or yarn to each origami. Then they are ready to hang up.

Posters:

Make origami from large squares for dramatic posters.

Table Decorations:

Fold a large index card (4 by 6 inches) in half. Glue an origami on the front.